mariposa x guerrera

Kim Guerra

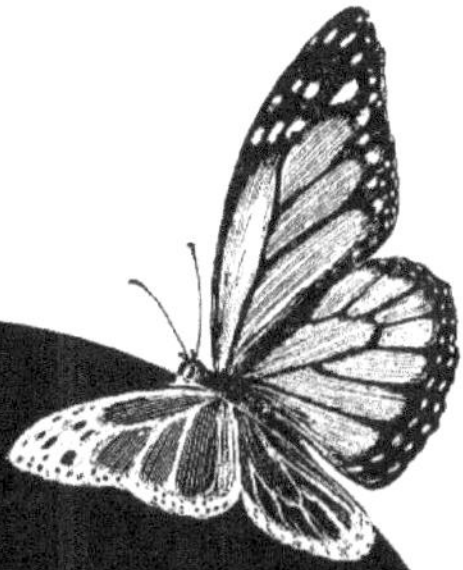

mariposa x guerrera

Kim Guerra

Kim Guerra

Copyright © 2022 Mariposa X Guerrera.

All rights reserved. No part of this publication may be reproduced, distributed without the prior written permission of the publisher, except in the case of brief quotations embodied in critical reviews and certain other noncommercial uses permitted by copyright law. For permission requests, write to the publisher, addressed "Attention: Permissions Coordinator," at the e-mail address below.

kim@brownbadassbonita.com

ISBN: 978-1-7379927-7-6
Library of Congress Control Number: 2022902138

Published by Alegria Publishing
Book cover and layout by Sirenas Creative

Mariposa X Guerrera

For all the niñas who are now mujeres
learning to love themselves.

Kim Guerra

Foreword

My writing has always been a reflection of my growth. It keeps me company as I heal and learn. It is part of how I love. My writing is como *vaporu* para mi corazon as it heals. It's become vaporu for the community as we heal and grow wings together. I write what I need to hear and no one is saying. I write for my inner niña- la que se sentía solita y se quedaba calladita. I write for the mamis and abuelas who didn't have the privilege of healing and loving themselves without guilt. I write for the ones with unresolved, intergenerational trauma who are now ready to heal.

"Mariposa" is a reflection and invitation to a metamorphosis. These poems were my medicine as I learned to love myself enough to give myself wings. It starts with you believing you are worthy of healing and deciding to live accordingly. Most of my life, I believed the only way I was loveable was when I was calladita y obediente. I lived to make everyone else happy. My life changed when I finally decided to love myself. It truly gave me wings. My hope for you is that you choose to love yourself enough to heal and give yourself wings, mariposa. May these words be a healing balm for your corazon. May this be an invitation to fly.
Mujer, eres una guerrera. You may not have had someone to fight for you when you were growing up. It's time you fight for yourself: your dreams, your needs, your wings. You are worth fighting for. Como dice mi abuela: *mereces lo mejor, no chingaderas*. Ámate con ganas.

We wanted to bring a revised version of Mariposa to life. We added new poems which were originally intended to be a part of the "Mariposa" collection. We also removed certain phrases and words which no longer align or fit well such as the word "womxn" (which was intended to be a more inclusive word for trans women. We have learned it is still excluding or "othering". Trans women are women. Y ya.) I've also added the term Latine to some of the poems which serves as a nonbinary way to identify with our cultura. I hope my writing continues to reflect my growth as I evolve, learn, and unlearn.

A volar se a dicho, mariposa!

Mariposa X Guerrera

Kim Guerra

Mariposa X Guerrera

I am loving myself
Into a garden.

Kim Guerra

Silence is no longer your home
-- Truth

Mariposa X Guerrera

She has light in her eyes and
Gold in her heart.

Kim Guerra

A lot of us are stepping out of
Internalized oppression and
Into radical self-love
-- liberation.
We are reclaiming the magic of our melanin.

Mariposa X Guerrera

Siempre me han llamado las flores
Como un lenguaje
Colorido, fluido.
Solo entre ellxs y yo.

Mis alas desnudas
Cuentan mi historia
desnuda
Como la verdad
Que me dio el valor y
Las ganas de volar

Mariposa X Guerrera

Today someone told me I don't look Latina.
What do Latines look like?
We look like seeds conquistadores couldn't bury.
We are golden like the sun.
Our laughter fills this world like fields of girasoles.
We are one and we are many.
Somos raza y familia.
So, yes I look like a Latina.
Me rio como Latina,
¡Porque soy Latina, y qué!

Cuídate a ti misma.
Amaté, eres una estrella fugaz.
Alumbras la noche con tu luz.

Mariposa X Guerrera

Women of color know what it's like
To have brown skin, big dreams, and a corazón
That keeps saying,
"Si *se puede.*"
Our works tell me,
"Si *se puede.*"
We must link arms, hold hands,
And remind one another,
"Si *se puede.*"

Kim Guerra

Hold yourself
Like you'd hold a flower.
Be in awe
Of your own beauty
The time you've taken to grow
The healing power
Held within your color
The sweet aroma of
A being determined
To bloom.

Mariposa X Guerrera

White fragility/Tears of color/Fall upon you/Acid rain on/White skin/You shatter
Glass/Struck/By truth/People /Different/From you.
You become/Glass shards/Cutting/People like me.
Glass /Under our skin.
You get mad at us for/Bleeding.
White fragility:/You demand we heal you.
You demand/We put you back together/With our silence.
You demand/We appease/Your temper tantrums.
You demand/We sugarcoat
Our/blood/color/Skin/Truth/For you.
White fragility:/You demand/We heal/So you/Feel better.
White fragility:/You do not know/Generational trauma/On your back/In your eyes/
The taste of your tears.
You do not know/Melanin magic/On your skin/ Treated like Disease.
You ask us to tell you/Then shut/Your ears/ Too much, too much/You shatter/ Once more.
White fragility:/You attempt to shame me.
I stopped caring for you./ I started caring
For me/For my people.
Until you too start caring/You will keep
Shattering/Each time/You hear
Our voices/Grow louder
Your whiteness/Will remain /Shattered.
White fragility:/Our lives have always mattered.
Our lives/Our stories/Our futures/Matter.
Until/White fragility
Becomes/White ability/There will be/No Unity.
Two cannot become one/If one/Demands/ Death/ Silence/Shame/Of the other
White supremacy.
Until/White tears/Weep with tears of color/ This

land won't heal.
Our tears like rain/Can heal each other.
Our hands/Our power/Our voices.
Until there is space for every race./Until all voices/
Are heard./Without being questioned/For validity/
White fragility.

Mariposa X Guerrera

Amanecí desnuda como el sol
Loca como la luna
Brillando como la luz.

Kim Guerra

I've realized part of growing up:
letting people go.
It's holding yourself close.
It's choosing over and over to love yourself--
Even when it's hard, uncomfortable, and unfamiliar.
Love yourself, even when it hurts.

Part of growing up: calling people out
For not treating you the way you deserve.
This first requires you to learn
How you deserve and would like to be treated.
It requires valuing yourself.
Valuing yourself means
Knowing and respecting
Your self, strengths, story
Truth, and beauty.

Mariposa X Guerrera

My energy is good,
My energy is light
My spirit is powerful.
I'm quick to stay away
From vibras negativas.
My light is far too valuable.

Kim Guerra

I write for the women learning to love themselves. I write for those blamed for being abused. I write for the one who was told to get over it. For those who were made to feel ashamed, I write for you. I write for those labeled as "bitter" for refusing to pretend nothing happened. I write for those too scared to speak up. I write for those forced to live with their abusers. I write for those who were told to smile and be nice. I write for those who were told, "Siéntate en mi pierna." I write for those who were told to keep secrets ever since they were little niñas—for those who are still keeping secrets. I write for women. I write for those who were abandoned by their families— because they broke the silence. This is for those asked to carry their family's lies. I write for the one who cries and cries. I write for the women who refused to let a single tear fall. I write for those clutching their pillow at night—for those who didn't dare open their eyes. I write for women. I write for the lonely niñas who are now lonely mujeres—for you who rise every morning a little bit stronger. I write for those who are healing. I write for women. I write for those who have nightmares, pesadillas durante la noche y el día. I write for those who yelled, "Stop!" and for those who barely let out a whisper. I write for the ones too traumatized to say anything at all. I write for those in therapy trying to put the pieces back together. I write for those who are too scared and need a hand to hold. I write for those who said, "A mí también. That happened to me too." I write for those with PTSD—for those starting to trust again. I write for those afraid to love, afraid of men, afraid of commitment. I write for those who are struggling to forgive— themselves, abusers, and those who didn't protect them. I write for women. I write for those whose Mamis were and are married to abusers, oppressors, cowards, drunkards, liars, aggressors—for those whose mamis chose to stay. I write for those whose Mamis forgot or never learned to be a mami. I write for the mamis looking out for their hijes so it doesn't happen to them. I write for the mamis who fought and are fighting for their daughters. I write for those who know. I write for women learning to love themselves—for those who overcame. I write for you who are loving yourself into a garden. I write for you and me.

Kim Guerra

If you are a white person--
A privileged person,
Especially if you are Christian,
You need to be doing everything
In your power
To stop the injustices
Occurring right now:
Deportations, Muslim bans,
any and all phobias of certain people groups,
Racism, sexism, oppression.

You need to use your privilege, time, voice,
And resources to fight
For freedom and equality--
Use your privilege to find the missing and murdered
Indigenous women, Black women, Trans women.
Raise awareness.,
Do something.
Try.
Fucking try.

What hurts the most:
We don't see you trying.
We don't see you at all
when it comes to our causes.

It's more than politics--
It's about

        Hue
        Man
        Ity
Saving   Lives
        And
        Lov
        Ing
        Peo
        ple

Mariposa X Guerrera

My body is like my heart:
Soft and full of love.

Mi cuerpo es como mi corazón:
Tierno y lleno de amor.

Kim Guerra

I am a privileged Latina.
This is hard for me to say.
My light skin, education, and citizenship.
Somehow, it made me feel less Latina.
Then, I learned I could use
My privilege pa' mi raza,
Mi voz pa' mi raza,
Mi vida pa' mi raza.
This is what being Latina is about.

Mariposa X Guerrera

Our struggles are many;
Our struggles are different.
I got your back, and
You got mine.
Above all,
We got each other.
Pa' mi gente.

Kim Guerra

When I'm with my people,
Mi gente,
There's an overwhelming
Sense of belonging.
I don't find this anywhere else.
There's a tight, unbreakable bond
Held together by
Ancestral blood
Running through our veins.
Nuestra cultura, nuestras palabras,
Y nuestros colores nos unen
Como nuestra misma sangre.

Mariposa X Guerrera

When I pray
I ask to be reminded of
Who I really am.
I pray the same for you
May you know the real you
May you look in the mirror
And see
Magic.
Your magic is real,
It's bright
Como las estrellas
Como la flor
Con tanto amor.

Kim Guerra

I decolonize and fight the patriarchy
Through poetry, art, and actions.
I resist and fight for justice
With my soul.

Mariposa X Guerrera

Resistance is part of our magic.
We resist by resting.
Our joy is resistance.
Our love is resistance.
Nuestra voz es resistencia
En un mundo que prefiere vernos calladas.
Resiste, mujer mágica.
Te necesitamos.

Kim Guerra

I pray we are reminded of the glory
Living within us.
I believe God is love.
Whatever isn't love,
Isn't God--
This too, I pray
My soul remembers.

It ain't the fluffy kind of love.
It's the blood, sweat, and tears
Kind of Love.
It's the ride or die
Kind of Love.
It's the love that stays
When you are covered in shame.
The Love that's too good to believe,
Yet your soul does anyway
Because we kind of need
That kind of Love.

Mariposa X Guerrera

While I was in México,
I felt the chasm between culturas.
Mexicans see me as American.
Americans see me as Mexican.
Ni de aquí, ni de allá.
Stuck in a canyon of cultures
That raised me,
I accepted the warmth of my third cultura:
Soy de aquí y de allá.
We've become a blanket and bridge
Between culturas.

Kim Guerra

Imperfections make us human.
Let yourself be human today.

Mariposa X Guerrera

People who hide from the truth,
Have not tasted freedom.
Those who pretend life is perfect,
Are too afraid to see their imperfections.
Until you accept your imperfect self,
You will not truly love yourself.
It's hard to love others when
You can't love yourself.

This is why I celebrate my imperfections.
I will always choose truth over pretense.
This is how I can love myself
And others freely.

Kim Guerra

One of the most beautiful things about
Latine people is
The generosity and hospitality
We were raised with:
Give and receive.
We come bearing gifts
And enjoy giving them:
Pozole in a tupperware,
Tamales,
Un dinerito pa que te compres algo nice,
A dozen eggs from mi tia's friend's cousin's gallinas.
We are people that don't like to see
Empty hands or hear empty stomachs--
We like to fill them.

Mariposa X Guerrera

Many in this country have
Rejected and abused
Our hospitality, hard work, and generosity
But we keep on
Loving, working, and giving.
We hold our heads high and
Our hearts close.
Nos gusta cantar en vez de llorar.
We are a strong people.
We are resilient.
We are a beautiful gente.
Somos Latines.

Kim Guerra

It's hard to mess with a woman who loves herself.

Mariposa X Guerrera

I used to shrink
When white people were around.
My family would shrink.
We would whisper
because we were afraid of speaking
Spanish in front of them.
What if they told us to go back
To our country?
What if they told us, "This is America.
Speak English!"
We were afraid of being separated,
So we assimilated.
Now, we take up space.
We aren't afraid.
We are here to stay.
We are on stolen land
The only illegal ones are the colonizers.
So, now I tell you:
Take up space.
Be proud of your big, brown family.
Habla Español.
Simply be your beautiful, Latine self.

Kim Guerra

I am a product of migration
Como las mariposas
Mi mami cruzó fronteras
Her own chrysalis
Risking her life
For her dream of flying
Su sueño de alas
For her dream of living
Sin miedo
For her dream of living
With liberty and justice
For all.

Things I'm learning:
- Brown skin is beautiful (so beautiful people pay money to get their skin to look like yours)
- Your body will always belong to you (this means you get to make all the rules)
- Fix things when they are broken instead of throwing them away (yourself included, relationships included)
- Trust actions more than words (love is something that is felt and done, not just said)
- Love is a choice that must start with you (a choice you must make everyday)
- You are more than just a body: you are a mind, heart, soul, and spirit (find a balance; nourish and care for every part of your being)
- Courage can save your life

Kim Guerra

For all the muxeres
Who were told
"De esas cosas no se habla"
For the ones they tried to silence
For the ones they tried to blame
You, mujer, are a fucking miracle.
Roar.
Dance.
Laugh loud in their face.
Grow.
Spread your arms
Como si fueran floreces
Creciendo.
Open your heart
Like the rising sun.
You are powerful.
You are here.
You are alive.
You are loved.
Your voice is necessary.

Mariposa X Guerrera

What does humanity look like?
You and me.
What does immigration look like?
You and me.
What does resilience look like?
You and me.
What does hope look like?
You and me.
What does change look like?
You and me.
What does love feel like?
You and me.

Mujer, eres única.
No tengas miedo de
Amarte a ti misma.
You are worthy.
You are beauty embodied.
Every part of you
Lonjitas and all--
Arrugas, verrugas,
Peluda and all--
Berrinchuda, enojona,
Llorona and all.
Eres única.

Mariposa X Guerrera

Mija,
I want to show you my world mi cultura, nuestra cultura. Nuestra comida y nuestras canciones. Our beautiful español. Quiero que conozcas el Amor: to love and not be afraid of loving. Whoever you choose to love. I want you to feel safe, worthy, confident enough to receive love the way you deserve to be loved. I want you to know, I will always choose you first— No man, struggle, or anything in this world can come between us—Absolutamente nada, mija.
Mija I was created to love you, protect you. Give my life up for you. You are my child, mija.
Made from my heart, blood, soul, body— yet you are your own person. I also love that about you. God trusted me enough to love you and raise you. This world is blessed to have you.
Mija, be kind. Keep your mind and heart open so fear doesn't come in. Mija, eres hermosa
in every way. You are beautiful. Mija eres fuerte. You can do all things. You have a stubborn ass mama and all of heaven cheering you on. Mija, be the kind of human that loves well.In order to do this, you must first learn to love yourself. I hope I love myself well enough that you can learn from me how to love you. Then, you can love others freely and fully. If someone is hungry, feed them. If someone is naked, clothe them. If someone is lonely, hold them. You will always have enough. You will always be more than enough. Mija be brave. Courage and resilience runs in our veins. Nuestros ancestors were warriors, los más valientes! Siempre le echaron ganas, they taught us: *si se puede*! Mija, we come from Aztec blood, mighty warriors, lovers, and protectors. Mija, we are seeds, nopales, mariposas valientes y resistentes. Mija, grow and love and love and grow. Do not be afraid to be beautiful. Do not be afraid to shine. Mija, I promise to

love you with unconditional, never-ending love. Mija, I promise I will mess up, make mistakes, and never ever be perfect. Mija, I promise I will learn, keep trying, and never ever give up. Mija, I promise to love you for who you are and not for who you "should" be. Mija, life isn't perfect or always pretty, but it is beautiful and worth living it with all we got. I will be there with you every step of the way. Mija, I will show you Love through my life and actions. Love will show itself to you. You are glorious. Eres tuya.

Mariposa X Guerrera

Woke up this morning to
Happy Birthday TuPac Shakur
Rest in Peace Philando Castile
Celebrating one's birth
And mourning another's death.
Two beautiful black men
Killed by an
Unjust
Oppressive
Racist
Violent
System
Created by white men
Too afraid of melanin
Too afraid to love black people
Too afraid to see them as humans
Equal to themselves.
Happy birthday, 2pac.
Rest in Peace, Philando.

Nosotros somos bougainvilleas
Wild, thorny, growing.
We embrace walls and cover them
With our resilience
Our ganas de crecer.
We grow until there are more of us
Than there are walls.
More flowers than borders.
Nosotros somos bugambilias
We grow together
Brilliant and loud.
You can't miss us,
Magenta flowers
Yelling,
"Here to stay!"

Mariposa X Guerrera

Fijate
Que vales las pena
Tus sueños valen la pena
Tu sonrisa vale la pena.
Fijate
Que la gente te va a fallar
Pero tus ganas y corazón
Seguirán latiendo.
Fijate
Que eres fuerte
Eres valiente
Eres soñador.
Fijate
Que mereces amor
Del bueno
Que tu vida importa
Que no estás solo.

Kim Guerra

I'm starting to feel most beautiful
When I am naked
And I stop trying to hide.

Mariposa X Guerrera

Mira, bonita
Chin up.
Dig your roots deeper
Keep growing
Each day you glow a little more.
Eres chingona.
Every bone in your body is
Badass.
Good and bad days
Your light will keep shining.
You are generations of
Sun soaked, brown skin.
Melanated mujeres
Went before you
So you can be standing here
today.

Kim Guerra

How can I celebrate/ The country that/ claims/ Justice and liberty for all/ When red blood from/ Black bodies/ Covers the streets./ Their oppressors run free./ No justice/ No liberty/ When Brown people/ My people /Are torn from their families/ In our ancestor's lands/ Deported and robbed/ No justice/ No liberty.
How can I celebrate/ When Muslim people/ Are being threatened/ Banned/ Because of their faith/ No justice/ No liberty./When LGBTQ communities/ Are being bullied and murdered/ Dehumanized/ because of who they love/ No justice/ No liberty. When pre-existing conditions/ Endanger people's lives/ Due to dwindling healthcare/ No justice/ No liberty.
How can I celebrate?/ This is not the land of the free./ This is not freedom./ I am not free/ until all are free./ This is a country/ Immigrants and refugees/ Called home/ The oppressed then/ Became the oppressors./ This land belongs to/ the Brown people massacred in the name of Justice and liberty./ This 4th of July,/ I will not celebrate./ I will mourn and remember./ I will acknowledge we have a long way to go/ until we reach/ justice and liberty/ For ALL.

Mariposa X Guerrera

Sometimes the strongest thing you can do is stop trying to be so strong.

Kim Guerra

Because you are a woman,
You are strong.
You are strong,
Because you are a woman.

Mariposa X Guerrera

Even when this nation tries to keep caterpillars from becoming butterflies
We will fill the sky with the sound of our wings.
Our radiant orange will outshine the rising sun.
Ellos temen que estas semillas color tierra,
Morenas como las montañas se convertirán en campos de girasoles.
Somos semillas guerreras
Crecemos y luchamos.
El sol es nuestra fortaleza y la lluvia nos alimenta.
Nuestras raíces son tan ondas como el mar y ancianas como las estrellas.
Y aunque intenten arrancarnos de nuestras tierras, seguiremos
Convirtiéndonos en girasoles
Y como monarcas llenaremos los cielos
Con nuestras alas
Como el sol seguiremos
Brillando, creciendo, luchando
Volando.

Kim Guerra

It takes courage to love yourself.
It takes self love to not be threatened by another woman's beauty.
We shine brighter together.
Let's glow up as a collective
Of women radically loving themselves.

Mariposa X Guerrera

Our ancestors worked the in the fields
And hustled the streets
So we could go into the academic fields
And reclaim our streets.

Summer in LA:
Calor y sudor
Comida
Elotes, raspados, paletas
Sol y playa
Puro party
Familia
Carne asada
Aguas frescas
Tacos y tortas
Callejones
Amigues
Memorias
Risas
90s songs
Chanclas
Atardeceres
Tu dime que más

Mariposa X Guerrera

I believe all shades of Brown are beautiful.
Our society does not.
So as a lighter-skinned Latina, I have to be quick to acknowledge my privilege.
I cannot claim to have the same level of oppression and discrimination as my darker skinned sisters.
If I were to do this, I would be disclaiming their narratives and invalidating their experiences.
I would be oppressing my sisters.
This applies to other communities of color as well, no solo Latines.
As a lighter skinned woman of color, I owe it to my darker sisters to own my privilege, check myself, and validate their voices.
I don't believe in skin tone policing.
Worry about loving yourself and empowering one another.
Own your privilege, love your skin,
Keep being a badass bonita.

Kim Guerra

I came from humble beginnings,
Deep roots kept me low to the ground.
My bare feet are blessed by madre tierra.
I am rising,
Yet I will never forget where I come from.

Mariposa X Guerrera

My hood shaped me,
So I could back and shape it
for the next generation of hood kids like me.

Kim Guerra

There's something about owning your roots
And owning your glow up--
Your achievements,
Your lucha,
Your victory.
As we rise,
Bring others up with you.
You make your parents proud,
You make your ancestors proud.
Stay grounded and never forget
Where your roots are planted.
Que no se te olvide la tierra
Que te dio vida.
Be a proud
Hood Girl Rising.

Mariposa X Guerrera

Latines in higher education have been told to shrink, assimilated, blend in

Marias baptized into Marys
Joses into Joes
In unholy classrooms.
Accents have been silenced, mocked, and whitened out.
Our lunches went from tacos to pizza.
Mami to the cold and hard "Mom"
Classrooms have been colonized
Massacres occur daily
As immigrants are bullied
Walls are built
Prison pipelines enslave our youth.
We are told, "Go back where you come from."
When at home our mami's and papi's
Tell of stories of how they got here
And why they risked it all to be here.
They remind us of their sacrifices and
Daily luchas.
So we could do better
Get an education.
Now that we are in higher education
Getting scholarships
Getting degrees
Getting the job done
We are learning to decolonize the classrooms
That oppressed us.
We are speaking up with trembling
Sometimes beautifully accented voices.
We are challenging stereotypes
Breaking down walls
Adding color to white washed
Oppressive institutions.
We are learning to challenge systemic racism
Empowering other people of color.
Latinx in higher education
Showing up every day

Mariposa X Guerrera

Making the
Si Se Puede
Our parents taught us
A reality.
The *si se puede*
Our parents crossed borders for.

Sana, sana alma mía.
Alma de mariposa.
Sana, sana alma mía
Si no sanas hoy,
Sanaras mañana.

Mariposa X Guerrera

Growing up, we didn't have much money
But we were rich in cultura.
This is a git I don't take for granted,
Especially now as an adult.
I see the importance of our cultura
Passing it down, embracing it,
Celebrating it, and letting it empower us.
It is a legacy of
Si Se Puede.
We are not going anywhere but up.
We are rising as our roots get deeper.
We bless the next generation when
we pass down the gift of cultura.

Kim Guerra

People of color need to be given priority.
Our lives need to be valued more than
White people's feelings.
If you are an ally,
You need to show up.
Protecting white people's feelings
Is what got us here in the first place.

Mariposa X Guerrera

We are seeds of resilience
Resistance is in our blood
Nuestra sangle cuenta historias
De lucha y victoria.
Now is the time children
Are standing up for their
Mothers and fathers.
Ancestors inspiring this generation
Of warriors.
Our voices are gathering
Strength.
We are becoming gardens and forests
Of revolutionary gente.

Kim Guerra

Mujer
You were taught to sacrifice your dreams
Yourself.
Mujer
It is time to rise and believe in
your dreams
yourself.
Mujer
You must learn to
Speak and fight for
Your dreams
Yourself.
Mujer
Teach yourself to love
Your dreams
Yourself.

Mariposa X Guerrera

Bañate en la tina
Ponte crema en las piernitas
Pon canciones de Selena
Prende unas velitas
Échate aceitito,
El que huela más rico
Desenrédate el pelo
No te cambies luego luego
Quédate encuerada un ratito
Escoge tu ropa favorita
Come bien
Píntate las uñas
Recuerda que eres hermosa
Sal a que te de el sol
Absorbe la luz,
brilla.

Kim Guerra

Mi mami's maiden name is Guerra.
It means war.
I come from a lineage of guerreras
Warrior women
Who overcame
Over and over again
Like the sun rises
Over and over again
So do the women en mi familia.
We have resting warrior face
Ready to slay
Anything getting in the way
Of justice, equality, freedom.
Libertad has costs us our lives
It requires humility to need each other
To call upon guerreras to walk beside me.
Your dreams will become my own.
Tu lucha es mi lucha.
Until we all are libre
Hasta que todes tengan justicia.

Mariposa X Guerrera

Part of my awakening
Was facing my internalized oppression.
Society made me believe the only way
I could be beautiful was to look like the White girls.
The only way I could sound beautiful
Was to talk like the gringos.
I used to be ashamed of not being white enough,
Skinny enough, rich enough.
My family was too Mexican,
Our butts were too big, we were too loud,
And we had just enough to get by.
As my eyes awoke
To the power and beauty of mi cultura,
They also awoke to
The racist in me--
The one who believed white was right.
The one who was ashamed of my skin, language, people.
Waking up means calling out
And unlearning internalized oppression.
Waking up means accepting and embracing
Mi cultura, lenguaje, y familia.
It means celebrating mi Latinidad, being a nalgona, and
Loving all the things I was taught to hate about myself.
Waking up, learning to see
Takes time.
Love yourself through the process.
Perdónate.

I was looking
At my little plant babies
Happy they were all so
Different
Beautiful
Unique.
They make the room more radiant
As they take up space and spread out
Their leaves
And deepen their roots.
As I was looking at my plant babies
With mad love
In my eyes
I realized God
Looks at us the same way.

Mariposa X Guerrera

May love be the heaviest burden on your back.
May love also be the thing that gives you wings.

Kim Guerra

If you need to cry,
Chilla.
If you want to fight,
Punch a nazi..
If you need to yell,
Grita.
Whatever you need to do to heal,
Do it.
You are worth it.
You are worth it.
You are worth it.
What's been done to you,
What's been taken from you,
Does not define you.
You are worthy of healing.
You are worthy of justice.
You are worthy of love.

Mariposa X Guerrera

Just a reminder that no one can take away
Our dreams, ganas, and lucha.
Resilient is who we are.

Kim Guerra

One of the best things you can do for yourself
Is to stop thinking about what others think.
It will give you wings.

Mariposa X Guerrera

To all the mujeres
Who are hurting
Who are healing
Who are reclaiming what was taken from them:
I see you.
You are the rising sun.
You are the ocean waves
Crashing, falling apart, and picking yourself
up over and over again.
You are making pearls
Out of grains of sand.
You are smoothing out the sharp edges
Of broken bottles and turning them into
Sea glass.
You are discovering you are the treasure.
You are rising and shining.
Your scars are turning into flowers.
You are becoming a home to yourself.

Kim Guerra

Never forget your roots.
They are the reason
You are blooming today.

Mariposa X Guerrera

Feed your soul.
We are spiritual beings.
When you feel empty
When likes, followers, money
Don't fill you up.
It's the spirit talking.
Listen.
May your spiritual life be a garden
Not a desert.
When I feel alone and empty
I turn to the Spirit.
The one who comforts,
The one who doesn't run out.
I've been close to giving up lately.
I've been close to surrendering to the emptiness.
I've been close to losing my spirit,
But God whispers hints of hope
And brings drops of rain to my desert heart.

Kim Guerra

When so many are offended by those
Taking a knee during the pledge of allegiance
A simple reminder
Of the wounds still bleeding
It shows they value a flag
More than what the flag stands for:
Freedom, equality, justice
For all.
For *all*.
The flag would take a knee too if it could.
We the people are waking up.
We are demanding the rights
Our ancestors were denied.
We the people are no longer afraid.
This makes the flag defenders tremble.

Mariposa X Guerrera

Mujer, tú eres de las que no se rinden.
Eres guerrera,
Vencedora
Como las flores en el desierto.
Las flores saben renacer.
Sueltan sus pétalos muertos.
Descansan para seguir creciendo.

Kim Guerra

I am
Liberated.
Soy
Mujer.
Resilient.
Loved.
Chingona.
Sin verguenza.
Y qué?

Mariposa X Guerrera

What if I told you
You don't have to be strong.
You don't have to be perfect.
You don't have to be who they say you should be.
What if the true key to freedom
Was loving, accepting, and being
yourself?

Kim Guerra

As women, we were taught to endure, overcome,
and be strong.
As minorities, we are taught to defy stereotypes
and statistics.
We were raised to be and do more than our white
and male counterparts--
All while avoiding the labels: angry, loud, defiant.
We are not taught that we are enough--
Our skin, socioeconomic status, history, and gender
Are considered disadvantages.
I'm here to tell you:
You are enough.
Your skin is enough.
Your melanin is enough.
Your story is enough.
Your humanity is enough.
You don't always have to be tough.
You don't always have to have it all together.
Sometimes being strong is admitting you are
struggling.
Sometimes being strong is letting go.
Sometimes being strong is loving yourself
Just as you are.

Mariposa X Guerrera

My soul is in need of Love;
I grew up knowing God as Love.
Religion almost ruined that for me.
Pain and suffering almost took me out.
Racist evangelicals claiming Trump as the
Chosen one caused me to flip tables.
Loneliness, trauma, and heartache almost made me forget
what Love, joy, and freedom felt like.
Suffering can draw us nearer
Or it can inspire distance.
Religion can cause faith to die.
My spirit is in need of the Divine.
Throughout this time in the wilderness,
I found a gem:
Stop acting Christian.
The less Christian I act,
The more Christ-like I become.
Church is Spirit within us--
Not a building. Find God within you
En y con nosotros.
I no longer wish to fit the cookie cutter molds.
I no longer wish to appear perfect.
I no longer feel the need to judge or change people.
I've learned to see my own need, my own shit, my own brokenness.
I am no one to judge.
I am a beautiful mess of a woman,
In need of a loving God.

Kim Guerra

I want to be the type of woman
That makes people wrinkle their nose.
I want to be so free,
It makes people uncomfortable.
I want to have the courage
To do things others are afraid to do.
I want to understand
I can't make everyone happy.
I want to release myself
Of others' expectations.
I am responsible for myself.
I will live the life I've always dreamed of.
I will live as if I'm worthy of love.
I am free.

Mariposa X Guerrera

I decide what to do with my pain.
My pain doesn't decide what to do with me.

Kim Guerra

I
Am
A flower
That's decided
To
Bloom.

Mariposa X Guerrera

Sending love
To survivors
Whether you said
"Me too"
Or not.
You don't owe
Anyone
Your story.

Quiero volver a brillar,
Como el sol al amanecer.
Quiero bailar como rayos
De luz sobre el agua.

Mariposa X Guerrera

We are all born caterpillars,
Butterfly written in our DNA.
Not all of us dare
To enter metamorphosis or
Break out of our cocoon.
When we do
We become frightened
To spread out wings
And fly.
Mariposa, stop fearing your own
Beauty, freedom, and strength.
Mariposa, become the glorious creature
You were created to be.
Vuela, mariposa, vuela.

Kim Guerra

Growing takes time.
Being human
Means
Being imperfect.

Mariposa X Guerrera

Something sacred happens
When you decide
You are worthy of
Love.

Kim Guerra

The next generation of Black and Brown babies
Need Black and Brown humans
Who love themselves.
Oppressive systems have taught us
To think we are bad and unworthy.
The next generations
Need us to unshackle ourselves from
Internalized oppression.
We need us.
We need Black and Brown people
To love Black and Brown people.

Mariposa X Guerrera

Part of loving yourself,
Is letting go of everything
That's hurting you--
Preventing you from
Growing and glowing.

Kim Guerra

As a Latina, I was taught to be self-sacrificing.
As a Christian, I was taught to be self-sacrificing.
I was taught this is a form of love and honor.
I was told not to make selfish choices--
Things that would only benefit me.
Doing things "just because I want to"
Was not encouraged by my culture or faith.
I did things for the greater good, for my whole family,
For my parents, for my husband, for my sister,
for my brother,
For my prima, for my aunt I met that one time when I was two years old,
For my neighbor, for my neighbor's neighbor, etc.
I was not encouraged to do things just because
They would make me happy.
I am learning to make choices for myself.
I will have to retrain my brain to not feel ashamed
For being happy.
Almost as if my life was just as important as theirs.

Mariposa X Guerrera

How will I love myself today?
-- a revolution.

I'm doing things that used to make me say,
"I've always wanted to, but..."
-- courage.

Mariposa X Guerrera

I always wanted to be like Frida.
I met her art when I was in high school.
Me enamore.
I felt connected to this mujer.
Sentí su corazón en el mio.
I felt her heart in her paintings, writing,
Letters, y en su mirada.
I saw myself.
Mi corazón en ella.
What I'm beginning to realize is:
I also felt her suffering.
It looked and tasted like mine.
Her loneliness.
Nuestra soledad y sufrimiento tienen
Los mismos colores.

Kim Guerra

The pain got to be too much for me
To carry by myself,
En silencio.
So, I began to write and create.
Even then, sufría.
So, I mustered the courage
To share.
I invited people to see, hear, and read me.
In some ways, I felt less alone.
The pain no longer lived solely within me.
It was out floating into the world and
Maybe held by those with similar pain--
Those who felt my heart in theirs.

Mariposa X Guerrera

Her pain didn't stop
She just turned it into art.

Kim Guerra

It is time to not give a fuck
About cosas que no valen la pena
It is time to luchar
For things that are worthy
-- like ourselves.

Mariposa X Guerrera

Frida was lonely.
She is powerful.
She let her pain
transform her
Into una mujer:
Chingona,
Fuerte,
Resilient,
Valiente.
She gave her suffering hell,
Fought and embraced
Her sorrow,
And she refused to
rajarse.

Kim Guerra

During times of loneliness and grief
I've learned to hold myself.
I found the strength to love myself.
The courage I needed to fly found me
Directo del corazón
I learned to make myself laugh,
Take myself dancing, and
Fight for the woman I am.
I've learned to hold on to me.
I almost lost myself--
Instead, I held on to me.

Mariposa X Guerrera

Make space
For your
Cultura.
It is
Sacred.
It is
A collection
Ancestors and stories
Music, language, food
Composing the elements
Of your
soul.

Kim Guerra

Listen to your body--
It has a lot to say.

Mariposa X Guerrera

You are loved.
Just as you are.
For what you are
And what you are not.
You are worthy of love:
To love and be loved.

En nuestra cultura
Our grief is a slow dance
Between songs and sorrow
Tequila y canciones
Aunque Frida nos advirtió
Tequila teaches our sorrow
To swim, not drown
Sentimos el dolor
Como olas del mar
Cantamos
Voz alta
Como relámpagos en las montañas
Las lágrimas
Aguas benditas que sanan heridas
Ondas como los ríos del ayer
Nos desahogamos con nuestro llanto
Nuestro canto
Así que llora y canta
Canta y llora
Alma mía
Que algún día volverás a
Reír y bailar.

Mariposa X Guerrera

I am grateful for my
Growth
Resilience
Struggle.
I am grateful for those
Who helped me
Along the way.

Kim Guerra

Raíces nuevas como manos
Enterrándose en la tierra
Desarraigando cadenas
Que algún día fueron llamadas raíces.
Ahora, rechazando la idea
Que la opresión será
La comida que alimentara
A nuestros hijos
Las generaciones por venir.
Raíces como manos
Trabajando en los campos
Liberando a humanos
Encadenados
Por racismo, machismo,
Odio a la diversidad.
Raíces como brazos
Deteniendo a los caídos
Apoderando a los que
Están amaneciendo
Abriendo sus ojos
A la injusticia
Raíces como alas
Dando el valor
Para luchar por todos
Para amar a todos.

Mariposa X Guerrera

Your womanhood is your power.
Your melanin is your magic.
Your joy moves mountains.
Your spirit is eternal.
No one can take that away from you.

Kim Guerra

Tu puedes.
Remember who you are.
Eres la victoria de tus ancestros
Solo por existir.
Whatever your battle
Whatever your dreams--
Tu puedes.
The courage of a thousand generations
La luz of a thousand suns
Runs in your veins.

Mariposa X Guerrera

It is not a love story
About a boy and a girl.
It's a love story
About a girl and her soul.

Kim Guerra

Your
dreams
Are
More
important
Than
Your
Fear.

Mariposa X Guerrera

Going back to your motherland es un abrazo al corazón.
There are times you can only find yourself
By returning to your roots.

Kim Guerra

Today, I write about the fact that many can't go back.
I write for those who need that abrazo al corazón,
Those who have families outside the U.S.
A las que no pueden abrazar.
I see you.
I will fight by your side until there are no more
Sides, walls, or borders--
Until you too get your abrazo al corazón.

Mariposa X Guerrera

You have the power to heal.

Kim Guerra

How can a woman
That's been through so much
Still love so well?
It's a combination of
God and awakening.
It's a decision to see
my worth.
Because even though I've been through shit
I still know how to love.
The gold of resilience:
The kintsugi of the soul.
The gold filling the cracks
Made by a broken world.
The decision to not
Let brokenness win.
The desperate desire
To let love in.

Mariposa X Guerrera

Pronto serás libre mariposa
Pronto abrirás tus alas otra vez.
No te desesperes.
Espera el tiempo de tu creador.
Pronto volarás con tu alma de mariposa
Pronto sentirás el viento bajo tus alas
Pronto probarás la libertad.

I am loving myself into a garden.

Mariposa X Guerrera

Black lives matter.

+The originators of the hashtag and call to action, Alicia Garza, Patrisse Cullors, and Opal Tometi, expanded their project into a national network of over 30 local chapters between 2014 and 2016.

Kim Guerra

Sometimes people that judge you the hardest
Are the ones in most pain.
Hurt people try to hurt people--
Rise above
Offer love and compassion
To those attacking you.
Only light defeats darkness--
Love generously and passionately
Live generously and passionately.
The more aware we are of our humanity
The more we embrace the fact we aren't perfect,
The harder it becomes to judge others
For their imperfect humanity.
The more we allow ourselves to be loved
In our imperfect humanity
(by God, friends, family).
The more we can love ourselves and
The more we can love others without judgement.
We all deserve to be loved just as we are.

Mariposa X Guerrera

Sometimes tears
Are the purest form of
prayers.

Kim Guerra

Dear self,
I choose to love you.
I choose to believe in you.
I commit to the woman you want to become.
I will protect you,
Look out for you,
Value you, and
Fight for you.
No more self-sabotage or
Letting fear get in the way.
Be free, mariposa.
You are going to fly!

Mariposa X Guerrera

Last year emptied me
This year, I will fill up
Until I overflow
My spirit is ready
To begin again
My wings are spreading
I am flying.

Alma mía
Algún día
Tus lágrimas
Se convertirán
En girasoles

Mariposa X Guerrera

Que no se nos olvide
Some of our parents had to learn
A whole new language
In order to get a job to support us,
Our families.
Que no se nos olvide
Some of our parents and grandparents
Worked in the fields, were eloteros, paleteros,
tamaleras, or housekeepers.
Que no se nos olvide
That there is no shame in our parents' struggle,
They show us what
Courage, resilience, and sacrifice look like.
A veces se nos olvida how privileged we are
To receive an education, have jobs we enjoy,
Have rights, and resources our parents didn't.
Hay que ponernos las pilas y echarle ganas.

Kim Guerra

I am starting to dream of the world again.
I dreamt of seeing, feeling, and loving the world.
I stopped, because I had to start surviving
Instead of living and dreaming and loving.
I want and need to stop surviving.
I am dreaming of the world again.
The world is dreaming of me.

Mariposa X Guerrera

You know they love you
If they call you
mija.

Kim Guerra

The cracks in my heart are healing
Enough to
hold more love in.

This is the year
I rise.

Healing is a release
Of all that is holding us back,
Causing us pain.

Healing is the act of
Throwing
Ashes into the wind
Believing they will
Rise
Like a phoenix.

Mariposa X Guerrera

We are in this
together,
mujer.

Kim Guerra

Choose love,
Over and over again.
Choose love,
For the parts of you that are tired.
Choose love,
In those moments you feel
the light leaving your body.
Choose love,
Over resentment.
This world,
Your heart,
Need you to choose love
Like your lungs
Need the air you are breathing.

Mariposa X Guerrera

You are worthy of being loved.
You are worthy of good things.
You are worthy of peace.
You are worthy of being seen.
Your story, pain, life, and joy matter.
I pray your soul remembers this
In times you feel unseen.

Kim Guerra

I have love for the land that birthed my ancestors--
Mi mami, papá, abuelos, y abuelas.
La tierra que nos dio
Nuestra cultura y comida--
Mangos, aguacate, maíz.
La tierra que nos dice,
"Canta y no llores."
I am honored to trace my roots
To the rivers and sierras of my motherland.
Siento la fuerza de mi gente
En mi sangre,
La dulzura dorada del sol en mi piel.
There are no walls or presidents
Que puedan quitar mi orgullo
Que le puedan quitar la belleza a nuestras tierras y culturas.
No nos pueden quitar las fuerzas ni las ganas.
No nos quitarán el sol de nuestra piel
Ni las canciones de nuestros corazones.
Seguiremos luchando y bailando nuestros bidi bidi bom boms
Seguiremos celebrando y amando nuestra
Tierra, gente, y cultura.

Mariposa X Guerrera

Many of us come from mamis who became
mamis when they were teenagers.
Mi mami was a seventeen year old
Learning a new language and cultura
In this foreign land.
Her mama wasn't there for her
She had to decide
Whether to raise a baby on her own.
I was a growing secret
Hiding under baggy, 90s sweaters.
I was a growing secret.
Yo era el secreto al que mi mami le cantaba
"Angel Baby" by Rosie and The Originals.
As I grow up, I realize the courage it takes
To become a mother.
Many of us have the privilege to have been raised by
Brave, badass niñas who became mamis
Who raised the brave, badass mujeres
We are today.

Kim Guerra

You are worthy of living
Without constant fear.
You are worthy
Of carefree laughter.
You are worthy
Of being cared for.
You are worthy
Of having valid feelings and needs.
You are worthy
Of love.

Mariposa X Guerrera

"Calladita te ves más bonita."
Desde chiquitas we are taught
Our silence equals beauty.
We are beautiful when we stay quiet.
"Lo que pasa en la familia se queda entre familia."
What happens in our home, stays in our home.
We were taught to fear our voice
Even when it carries the truth.
We were taught to protect others
Even when it meant sacrificing ourselves.
For all those valientes learning to trust
Their voice, their truth
I see you.
There is nothing more beautiful
Than the courage to love and speak up
For yourself.

Kim Guerra

Mujer, society raised you to be insecure
To hate your body, your hair, your curvas.
Mujer, you were raised to become a shadow
Following men as they soaked up all your sun.
Mujer, you were taught to become blind
To your own beauty and power.

Mujer, you were taught to take the blame
For everything under the sun
Without stopping to care for your aching back.
Mujer, you had to unlearn all those things
And teach yourself to love
Yourself.
Mujer, you began and became
A revolución.

Mariposa X Guerrera

Que vivan las mujeres
Sin miedo y con poder.
Que vivan las mujeres
Con derechos y libertad.
Que vivan las mujeres
Con paz e igualdad.
Que vivan las mujeres
Con oportunidades de amar
Y triunfar.

Kim Guerra

Decisions have terrified me
Most of my life.
So, I never made them.
Instead, I handed my decisions to
God, family, friends, anyone
But me.
I made them thinking of everyone
But me.
I was afraid of my voice--
Unwilling to take responsibility for
My own life.
I believed I was not worthy or strong enough
To be powerful.
We get one life, alma miá.
I hope you learn to love and trust yourself
Enough to live the life you deserve.

Mariposa X Guerrera

It takes courage
To listen to
Your
Corazón.

Kim Guerra

"You are going to have to free yourself," my therapist tells me.
"I don't know how," I whisper.
Tears climb up my eyes as I hold my cup of tea tighter.
To catch my tears if they fall.
"You were a defenseless girl, and now you are a powerful woman. It's time to empower yourself."
"It's not going to be easy, pero tu eres una guerrera," grita esta alma mía.

Mariposa X Guerrera

Querida mujer,
No estás sola.
No eres débil.
You carry light
Within your soul.
The one you need
To guide you out
Of the darkness.
The wilderness is a season
In which your chains are falling off
Your strength being renewed.
It's a time for your heart to break open
Enough to receive the love you
Desperately need.
Mujer, es tiempo de que te des cuenta
Que eres más que suficiente.
Mujer, eres digna de ser amada.

Kim Guerra

I grew up in and out of the neighborhoods
The white kids used to call "ghetto"
They joked about getting shot if they were to visit me.
I went to an Ivy League where people
Came from privilege I didn't know was possible.
One girl was online shopping in class
I gasped
She bought herself a $5000 purse
Just like that.
It was almost half a year's rent for my family.
It would have been easier to succumb to the odds
Against me,
But that's not me:
A brown, badass, bonita;
A hood girl rising;
La mujer que todo lo puede.

Mariposa X Guerrera

Dear Black women,
You are worthy of being celebrated every damn day.
As a light skinned brown woman, I can't claim to know
What it's like to walk in your shoes.
As I walk alongside my black sisters,
I notice the microaggressions, oppression, racism, and injustices
You have to navigate on a daily basis.
Your beautiful, rich, magical melanin
Has been disrespected for far too long.
You've seen your ancestors, fathers, mothers,
Brothers, sisters, and your people slaughtered by
The ones who were supposed to protect them.
I want to apologize for the anti-black and anti-dark skin
Narratives that have been passed down by my people.
Beautiful, black women I want to acknowledge
And express gratitude for the emotional labor
You've poured out to educate us about your experience.
You've had to convince people of why your life matters.
This is heartbreaking and inhumane.
You've have to fight harder than most of us to reclaim
Your history, stories, culture.
You keep getting robbed and condemned by white people
Who treat you as if they own you.
Yet, you shine in your magic and break down chains with your joy.
You are reclaiming and fighting for what has always been yours.
Black women, we need to celebrate the miracle you are every damn day.

Kim Guerra

Mujeres are also sexual beings
With their own desires and needs.
Mujeres were taught to suffocate their sexuality,
I am here to fan it into a flame.
Mujer, you no longer need to be afraid
Of your own body and desire.
Sex is not a dirty word,
It's time to reclaim it.
It's time to see
How sacred and breathtaking
You are.

Mariposa X Guerrera

To the boys and girls
Who were abused,
You are worthy of healing.
Many of us grow up internalizing oppression,
Believing we are worthy of being treated this way--
That somehow we deserve it.
It is time to tell your inner child:
It's not your fault,
You are worthy of love,
I am here to fight for you now.
We get to love the child within us,
Give ourselves permission to grow wings.

Kim Guerra

Resilient como las mariposas
That come into this world as
Wingless, crawling creatures.
Resilient como las mariposas
Creating for themselves
A chrysalis, a safe haven
And catalyst for change.
Resilient como las mariposas
Breaking through the shield that protected them
In order to emerge, evolve
Into the being they were meant to be.
Resilient como las mariposas
Fighting to fly
Spreading their wings
Finally touching the sky.

Mariposa X Guerrera

No confundas
La tristeza
En mi mirada
Con debilidad;
Cada día
Me hace más fuerte,
Cada lágrima
Sana las heridas
En mi corazón.

Kim Guerra

I want to be able to dispel shame
From my womanhood,
Cast out the shame
from my faith,
Leave shame out
Of my sexuality.
Instead, I want to
Celebrate my womanhood,
embrace a shameless faith,
Call my sexuality holy.

Mariposa X Guerrera

Internalized oppression is when we see our people
Through the oppressors' eyes.
We decolonize our cultural identity
When we see our people through our ancestors' eyes--
Con amor.
We decolonize our tongue when
We embrace our native languages.
El español es arte--
It adds to our beauty and power as a people.
Our cultura is a shield
Brillante, fuerte como el sol
Que nos da las fuerzas y ganas
Que nos hace the resilient and loving
Guerreras that we are.

Mujer te quiero ver
Amándote
Con todas tus fuerzas
Quiero verte sanando
Las heridas que has cargado
Por generaciones.
Mujer, ámate más cada día
Tu amor les enseñara
A los demás lo que mereces.
Mujer, sé el amor de tu vida.

Mariposa X Guerrera

I am unearthing my inner guerrera —
The warrior woman
I've always known
Lives within me.
The one who gave my maternal lineage
The last name
Guerra.
The one I was taught to fear —
The one who frightened men,
The one who caused oppressors to shake.
She is rising like the sun
Radiant,
unstoppable.

Alma mía,
I am fighting for you.

Mariposa X Guerrera

We are rising,
Embracing what it means to be
Latine,
Owning all that makes us
Badass,
Decolonizing our definition of
Bonita.

Kim Guerra

I am becoming more and more
Aware of the empty areas in my life —
The ones that need to be filled up.
It used to be an act of despair.
Now, I am grateful I know exactly where these areas are.
Before, I simply felt the ache of hunger in my heart.
I didn't know what it was hungry for.
Now, I am grateful.
Where there is a wound,
There is also an opportunity for healing.
I grew up wounded and blind.
I am learning to see.
I am learning to heal.
Here I am —
Bleeding, healing, breathing,
Being, seeing.
Here I am —
A miracle.

Mariposa X Guerrera

Unlike many women in my family,
I have the luxury and privilege of healing.
I have felt the wounds of these matriarchs.
I feel them deeply.
I am determined to break these cycles.
I am determined to reclaim our worth,
I am determined to reclaim our voices,
I am determined to reclaim our stories.
I am learning how to value myself.
I am learning to call my voice sacred.
I am taking my time to heal.
I am doing this for me.
I am doing this for my ancestors.
I am healing for my future children.
Our generation is moving from surviving
To learning to heal and love and fly.

Kim Guerra

I am learning to say, "No."
It is strange.
It is necessary.
It is growth.
Saying no does not mean I am selfish.
Saying no does not make me a bad person.
I am learning that saying no is part of my personal rights.
It is part of honoring myself and considering my needs
Just as important as other people's.
It is part of my revolution.

Mariposa X Guerrera

I used to want to change the world and make
 a name for myself.
Now, I just want to love the world and accept myself.
I've learned that is more than enough.

Kim Guerra

I am my own genre of mujer.
I am making my own rules
As to what kind of woman I want to be.
I am tired of fitting into boxes
That were originally created to oppress me.

Mariposa X Guerrera

I hate wearing a bra.

Kim Guerra

Power and revolution
Come from within.
I want to hear the sound of the chains
Called internalized oppression
Crashing on the ground
As we fight and liberate ourselves
And each other.
No hay de otra.
We hold the keys to break off the chains:
Self love and love for our people.

Mariposa X Guerrera

Your healing is worth your time.
Your voice is worth fighting for.
May you take the time to find your voice,
Use it until it becomes louder than thunder,
Brighter than lightning.
Your voice can change lives,
Starting with yours.

Kim Guerra

Mujeres somos guerreras.
Many of us weren't taught how to fight for ourselves.
We were made to believe we weren't worth fighting for.
We weren't given the tools:
Boundaries, self-love, confidence.
We've had to learn to make the tools ourselves.
We've had to unlearn the oppressive messages passed down
About our womanhood.
We've had to learn to love ourselves
Enough to fight for ourselves—
To believe we are worthy to call forth and embrace
The guerrera within each one of us.

Mariposa X Guerrera

Many will tell you, "No."
Be sure to tell yourself, "Yes."
Your dreams? "Yes."
Your growth? "Yes."
Your rights? "Yes."
Your needs? "Yes."
Your wants? "Yes."
You? "Yes."
Dite a ti misma que si y no le pidas permiso a nadie más.

Kim Guerra

I've been holding my breath a lot.
Uncertainty does that to you.
I've been exhaling prayers in between breaths.
Survival does that to you.
I've been holding my weary heart a little tighter.
Grief does that to you.
I've been loving myself a little more each day.
Hope does that to you.

Mariposa X Guerrera

Yo soy más
que suficiente.
This corazón,
these dreams, words, eyes, lips, hands
are more than enough.
The biggest way
I can disrespect myself
is by not embracing, loving, celebrating myself.
Mujeres, we disrespect
ourselves when
we compare ourselves
to others or try to be someone else.
You are more than enough.

Kim Guerra

Your dreams are sacred.
Protect them with your life.
Fight for them con ganas.

Mariposa X Guerrera

I chose to step fully into
the imperfection of my beauty.
I chose to open my eyes and see myself
for who I was, who I am,
and who I am becoming.
There is pain in my beauty
and beauty in my pain.
There is also a softness
resulting from years of suffering.
When you are in a desert,
desperate to feel loved,
you have two options:
perish or love yourself.
I am still here.
I chose to love myself
when I didn't feel loved.
I learned to call myself beautiful
and believe it.
I chose to find my power and
not let people take it from me.
This is my imperfect beauty.

Machistas are mugre.

Mariposa X Guerrera

Protect the niños not the guns.
We've had enough of this Amerikkka—
the one that promised opportunity for all
the one where dreams came true.
Now, kids are being shot in schools
and Dreamers are being deported.
We've had enough of this Amerikkka—
so, the kids are fixing what their parents broke
even while their wounds are still bleeding
and their friends are being buried.
We've had enough of this Amerikkka.

Kim Guerra

Mujer, levántate.
Rise up and realize
you are all you need
to turn your life around.
It's in your nature to create
give birth to new beginnings
Tu vida is your masterpiece.

Mariposa X Guerrera

¿Y qué?
—a proper response to almost anything

Kim Guerra

You will make it,
even if it takes all the strength you have.
You are like the sun,
rising each day and each day getting stronger.
You are like the moon,
light in the darkness.
You are like the stars being born,
and the supernovas releasing
all their brightness as they go.
Mujer, you are a galaxy:
sol y luna y tierra y mar.
Mujer, you will make it,
Vas a ver.

Mariposa X Guerrera

No te dejes, mujer.
We were taught to be calladitas,
obedientes, sacrificial.
We were taught to sacrifice ourselves—
to surrender our power
simply because of our gender.
Pero ya no.
We are learning to defendernos
luchar por nuestra vida, voz, y alma.
No te dejes, mujer.
Many will try to take your power,
pero no se te olvide: es tuyo—
y tú eres tuya.

Kim Guerra

I am finally taking time to see
myself.
I see beauty, strength, and resilience.
I see the battles my ancestors fought.
I see the battles I'm fighting.
I see the mujeres that came before me
and the ones yet to come.
I see me in the moments I felt forgotten.
I've found the pieces of me
I thought were lost forever.
I am reclaiming myself
by seeing and loving myself.

Mariposa X Guerrera

Selena, I often find myself thinking about
what it would be like if you were still alive.
Mis hermanitas y yo would watch the movie
about your life almost everyday.
We would put the VHS in the old tv in
and sit on the carpet in our chones.
Every time the white rose fell and
the gun was shot nos poníamos a chillar.
I still cry.
You showed us que niñas como nosotras
could be a mujer like you one day:
brave, talented, compassionate, y proud of her
cultura.
Your music and legacy continues to
empower us and bring us together.

Kim Guerra

Don't be afraid of wanting to be loved.
Don't be ashamed of giving yourself the opportunity to discover yourself.
Don't let anything or anyone stop you from growing: spiritually, mentally, emotionally.
You are worth it.

Apologizing for your light skin, won't do anything.
Own your privilege and be responsible.
It shouldn't be light vs dark skin within our own communities.
Colorism is a form of internalized oppression in which we oppress our hermanes.
Lift each other up, don't shame one another for having more or less melanin.

Kim Guerra

Our darker skinned and Afro-Latine hermanes
have been silenced and misrepresented for too long.
It's time to listen instead of getting defensive.
If a darker skinned sister is speaking:
listen.
Lighter skinned minorities don't face the same type of
oppression or discrimination.
We must own that and acknowledge it.
It's not a competition and if you view it as that you are
only stopping the revolution.
We must come together and lift up one another's
voices instead of trying to drown
each other out.
If our hermanes are sharing their
experiences, stories, struggles, victories, and success:
lift them up, empower them, be happy for them.
When one of us wins, we all win.

Mariposa X Guerrera

Corazón, I am listening.
I am your advocate and friend.
Te cuidaré y amare.
Corazón, gracias por no rendirte
por latir aun cuando no tenías fuerzas
por amar aun en la oscuridad.
Corazón, eres un milagro
directamente de Dios.
Corazón, vamos a amarnos.

Kim Guerra

Mujer, eres una guerrera.
Courage
runs through your veins.
You are not only a
survivor,
you are a
warrior.
Mujeres, you are worthy.
You've lived most of your life
living in shackles
because no one told you
you are a queen.

Mariposa X Guerrera

Nuestra cultura corre en nuestras venas,
es parte de nuestra belleza.
The world sees the richness of our culture,
the closeness of our people.
Our love, generosity, laughter, food, music
are all directo del corazón.
We are so damn powerful, mi gente.
The world tries to make us feel small
only because they see how great we are.

Kim Guerra

I can feel my decisions
informing
my growth.
My self love is
making me
glow.

Mariposa X Guerrera

You are a nurturer by nature.
Use the gift you've been given
to nurture yourself.
Pour in to yourself as if
you were someone
worth loving and investing in.
Treat yourself
like you would treat
a priceless treasure—
it's what you are.
Eres un tesoro,
cuídate y ámate.

Mujer, mírate a los ojos.
Déjate ver lo fuerte,
hermoso, y tierno de ti.
Learn to see your own beauty
and cultivate it on the daily.
Use your healing powers to
nurture yourself back to life.
Use your tenderness to
build yourself up again.
Eres una reina, un jardín, un tesoro.

Mariposa X Guerrera

Let yourself make mistakes.
Don't let fear stop you.
Give yourself the chance to
grow
and do things you never
thought you could.
Embrace
the challenges, waves, deserts
that come your way.
Give yourself the gift of strength,
the gift of growing brighter.

Dear future self,
I am choosing to love you today.
I am choosing to love you tomorrow.
I choose to love who you were ayer.
I choose you todos los días.
Nunca mas te abandonaré.
Eso si te lo prometo.

Mariposa X Guerrera

I wouldn't have survived if
I hadn't made the conscious choice
to love myself.

Kim Guerra

You love
and
you learn
and
You learn
and
you love
Until
Loving
Becomes
Learning
and
Learning
Becomes
Loving.

Mariposa X Guerrera

The world may lie
and tell you
you're alone—
but as long as you've
got God and
a beating heart,
you've got
all you need.

Kim Guerra

If someone makes you feel selfish
for loving yourself,
It's only because they haven't learned to
love themselves.
The truth is, you can only love others well
if you learn to love yourself first.
Nourishing, caring for, and taking time to
discover and meet your own needs
provides you with the emotional, mental,
spiritual, and physical resources to be a
loving presence to others.

Mariposa X Guerrera

Let yourself laugh loud.
Honor your fire and passion.
Give yourself permission to live
the life you've envisioned.
Respect yourself enough to
believe in yourself.

Kim Guerra

Queer
Trans
Black
Indigenous
People of Color
your presence alone
is a Revolution.

Mariposa X Guerrera

I am learning
what I have to say
is important,
because who I am
is important.

Kim Guerra

Don't forget you are a work in progress:
caterpillar,
chrysalis,
breakthrough,
Butterfly.
Sometimes we go through this metamorphosis
Over
And
Over
again.

Mariposa X Guerrera

Cuando nos cansemos
de quedarnos calladitas
that's when the
revolution begins.

Kim Guerra

We are still here.
We are still growing.
We are marching.
We are speaking up.
We are voting. We are graduating.
We are healing.
We are learning to take care of ourselves.
We are instigating change. We are fighting.
We are getting back up.
We are fearless.
We are resilient. We are the revolution.
We are liberating ourselves.
We are taking up space.
This is a testament to the resilience
that makes up who we are as a people.
No nos rajamos.
We believe in si se puede.
We are a living *si se puede*.
Yes we can,
and yes we will.
Because we are.

Mariposa X Guerrera

The first time someone told me, "Eres una guerrera" was when I was 25. I was leaving therapy and my therapist: a Cuban guerrera who looked me in the eyes and said, "You are going to learn to fight for yourself. Tú puedes, eres una guerrera." It made me wonder what my life would have looked like if mi mami had told me that message and if her mami had told her. Perhaps, there wouldn't be so many cycles of abuse and oppression present in our lineage.
I wasn't taught to fight for myself. Instead, I was told, "Calladita te ves mas bonita."
I was told to be quiet and to aguantar-- tolerate abuse in silence. This was one of my main roles as a mujer, hija, sister, wife.
"You are worth more than this. You are a warrior. Eres una guerrera, digna de lo mejor."
I didn't know how thirsty my soul was for those messages. It's like I had been waiting to hear them my whole life.

Kim Guerra

"Porque quiero"—
a revolutionary phrase
for mujeres.
We were taught to do things
for others, nunca for us.
So when they ask me why
I'm doing something and I say,
"Porque quiero."
It's like I insulted their mama.
They haven't learned that mujeres like us
have a right to do what we want.

Mariposa X Guerrera

When we honor the humanity in each other not only
do we show respect to the other person,
we show respect to ourselves.

Kim Guerra

There will be days
you need to be by yourself;
other days you'll need
your friends, mami, sisters, partner.
There are days when
you need to rise up
and days when
you lay low
even days when
you need to be on your knees
praying
you will make it through.
And guess what?
You will make it through.

Mariposa X Guerrera

Mujer
stand your ground.
Don't change yourself for another.
You've worked so hard to
find yourself
build yourself
love yourself
back to life.
Celebrate and protect the self
you've worked so hard to become.

Estoy creciendo
mis ojos abriendo
Me estoy descubriendo
amando lo que encuentro
dentro de esta alma amaneciendo.

Mariposa X Guerrera

A veces la vida nos lleva
a lugares que no podemos ver
solo sentir y confiar
que eso es suficiente.

Kim Guerra

Mothers
turn seeds
into
flowers.

Mariposa X Guerrera

Our mamás gave,
so we could receive.
This is love.

Kim Guerra

Be the kind of woman
other women can go to
without fear of getting judged
or shamed.
Be the kind of woman
that builds up and empowers
be a refuge and an overflowing well.
Be the kind of woman
that loves other women well.

Mariposa X Guerrera

Doing things just because you want to
is an act of self love.
It means you are paying attention
to your wants and needs
and considering them important.

Kim Guerra

Ahorita more than ever
necesitamos nuestra cultura
necesitamos las fuerzas de
nuestros ancestros.
We need to gather the resilience
they passed down to us.
We need to live out,
"Sí *se puede.*"
It is our turn to carry the fire
pave the way for the next generation
of Latine revolutionaries.

Mariposa X Guerrera

No te dejes.

Kim Guerra

Mujer, did you know
your inner self is sacred?
Your essence, soul, spirit
are worth more than gold.
Respect yourself as if you were
your most valuable possession.
Your dreams, energy, and time
belong to you
and you get to decide
with whom you share them.
Mujer, tu vida
es tu tesoro.

Mariposa X Guerrera

Mujeres nurture generations
Move mountains
Change nations.
No se te olvide, mujer
eres una fuerza imparable.
Tu eres el corazón
que hace girar este mundo.

People of color
Gente de valor.
People con melanin
gente con magic.
Gente revolucionaria
guerrera
luchadora
vencedora.

Mariposa X Guerrera

Find and free immigrant children.
ICE has lost 1500 immigrant children. ICE has also left children separated from their families in the hands of traffickers. There are other children being held in camps, sleeping on the floor, under constant maltreatment. This needs to stop.
I could have been one of those children.
That could have been mis hermanitos.
It breaks my heart to see how toxic this country and government is for immigrants, refugees, and dreamers.
We cannot be complicit with our silence.
Do not look away.
This is our family.

Kim Guerra

I am ready to put
my crown on again.
Estoy lista para recibir
lo que merezco—
amor, respeto, valor.

Mariposa X Guerrera

Momentos de soledad
Momentos de pensamientos
Tiempos de decisiones
Solo mías.
Esto es un privilegio llamado
independencia.
Mi voz por fin tiene importancia.
My voice will be the loudest
porque es mi vida.
Es la obra de arte que Dios me ha encargado.

Kim Guerra

Soy una flor.
Juntas, somos un jardín.
Cuidémonos.
Mujer,
I love watching you grow.

Mariposa X Guerrera

You are climbing mountains, mujer.
You are a river carving new paths
for yourself,
the women before you, and
las mujeres rising after you.
I pray we rise higher.
May our struggles and victories
become stepping stones for
the next generations
to climb higher mountains.

Kim Guerra

This man and I have had breakfast every morning for the past twenty years.
—Tapatio

Mariposa X Guerrera

One of the most
revolutionary lessons
I've learned is that
no matter what I do
or what I've been through
my value doesn't diminish.
I'm still a
motherfucking diamond.
Sigo siendo una reina,
my magic is still mine.
I am still worthy of love.
Yo soy la única que decide
mi valor.
Mi luz y alma
are worth
more than gold.

Kim Guerra

I am in the presence of royalty,
warrior women, survivors,
women bearing glory,
gold shining through the cracks,
turning wounds into divine scars.
Our spirits holding one another
as our stories intertwine, come alive.
Our hearts beat together
as we break chains, make change, and
share our courage with one another
—the gift of sisterhood.

Mariposa X Guerrera

There are days
when you will look
at a blooming sunflower
and say, "I know how you feel."

Kim Guerra

Pase lo que pase
aprenderás a levantarte.
Sometimes our greatest battle
is believing we are worthy
of receiving the love we deserve.
Pero when we do,
our whole world changes.
You no longer accept
excuses or anything other than
the kind of love
that reminds you:
You are a queen.

Mariposa X Guerrera

Cuando cometas errores
abrázate—
de esos apretados
que hacen que tus ojos se cierren
y tu corazón se acelere.
If we don't love ourselves
through our mistakes,
shame comes in.
Embrace yourself in those moments
look yourself in the eye
learn and fly.
Mujer, don't forget you are human.
You are allowed to be imperfect.
You are allowed to try again.

Kim Guerra

Growing up "la migra" was always a threat for my family. At a young age, mi mami explained to me that there was a chance she could be taken away. She would tell us what to do in case la migra took her. "Go to the neighbor's house and tell her to call your Tita," she would say. This was a constant fear we would carry with us everywhere we went. The children today are living out my worst nightmare. This has got to stop. Familias belong together. Let's do everything we can to keep familias together. Not in cages. Con alas. Libres. Juntes.

Mariposa X Guerrera

Keep your head up
remember you are the flor
that grew from the concrete.
You will keep growing,
mariposa seguirás volando.
You will keep learning
how flowers grow in the wilderness.
You are a wildflower,
growing against all odds.

Kim Guerra

I'm somewhere in between
a good girl
and a bad bitch.
Sometimes both
and that's okay.

Mariposa X Guerrera

FAMILIAS BELONG TOGETHER
Yet they are being torn apart
Niños llorando
children in cages.
It could have been us
you, me
mis hermanitos.
This is actually happening to our
hermanes.
To our Familia,
our resilient gente Latine.
Que nuestras
lagrimas, fuerzas, y lucha
nos unan.
Amen.

Kim Guerra

Ámate con ganas.
Ámate como si tú vida
depended on you
loving you.

Mariposa X Guerrera

It's a process—
loving yourself.
You will fall and fail—
go back to old survival skills.
Love yourself through that;
Fight the shame.
Get back up and rediscover your wings.
Mujer, you are learning to walk on your own.
You are going to put on that crown
and soar.
Your wings will become mosaics of
Sunsets, oceans, new horizons.
Love will become your friend.

Kim Guerra

Keep those who
add to your life;
Subtract those who
don't.
Your time and energy
are sacred.
It's simple math, really.

Mariposa X Guerrera

Preparing myself as a future
mental health worker
to work with the traumas
and wounds these children
will need to heal from.
We will heal each other
desde ahorita
juntemos nuestros
privilegios, power, y magia
prayers, skills, art
para sanar a nuestra
gente querida.

Let God love people through you.

Mujer
keep your standards high.
A veces people, spaces, and
internalized messages will try to
make you question your worth.
Pero acuérdate por lo que haz
luchado.
Remember the battles you've
fought and won
for yourself.
Acuérdate que eres una
reina.

Kim Guerra

Respira profundo.
Call the warrior women in your life.
Practice gratitude.
Ask yourself who is loving you well,
Be one of those people.
Remember your standards.
Hold your head high.
Rest and rise.

Mariposa X Guerrera

I've been using other people
to distract me from myself.
I've been scared to go and see
myself from within—
to touch the healing wounds,
the bleeding ones,
the scars.
I've been telling myself,
"I'm strong. I'm fine. Just keep going."
When my heart is saying,
"Stop.
Slow down.
Let me catch my breath."
Rest and solitude can be terrifying
when you are used to
hustling and surviving.
What happens when you need
rest and solitude to survive?
What happens when your heart
is asking you to fall in love with you
in order to rise?

Déjate disfrutar la vida
es tuya.
Si quieres andar greñuda,
anda.
Si te quieres arreglar y andar bien guapa,
anda.
You want to dance como La Chona?
Baila.
Vive por ti misma;
Vive like it is your vida
and no one else's.

Mariposa X Guerrera

You are using ancestral
wisdom and strength
to heal, build, restore
what they couldn't.
You are fighting breaking the chains
that oppressed them.
We are continuing their legacy,
picking up the torches they left us
para mantener la revolución viva!

Kim Guerra

The beauty of resilience is that it doesn't end.
You continue to learn, grow, and blossom.
There are days when you will be a seed,
others you will be the water, sun, earth, wind
You need to grow.
También tendrás días cuando serás
la flor y las raíces.

Mariposa X Guerrera

At times, the breaking begins with a small crack
which grows deeper, stronger, wider
until there is no more heart, no more love
solo piezas tiradas en el piso
enterradas como semillas
meant to help the next amor
become a flor.

Kim Guerra

Other times, a heart shatters
like a rock shooting through a window.
So sudden it takes your breath away,
you feel the million pieces cutting you from within.
They make you bleed
when you try picking them up
with your trembling fingers.
This kind of heartbreak leaves scars,
wounds that feel like they are never going
to heal;
that threaten to be eternal
and promise you will never love again.
But the bleeding will stop,
the wounds will heal,
You will find beauty in your scars,
And you will once again be brave enough
to fall and rise in love again.

Mariposa X Guerrera

The worst kind of heartbreak is the one
where the heart breaks over and over again
and is put back together with
false promises
desperate hope
fear of being alone.
The heart stops working like it used to
It doesn't beat the same
It's an empty shell
used as an excuse
to stay and call it love.

Kim Guerra

Reina,
Do not base your worth
on the attention of men.
Whether it is a lot of attention or not,
You do not need their approval—
you are still a Queen.
You do not need them at all—
you are still powerful, worthy, beautiful.
Reina eres inteligente y única.
You are lovely.
Protect your sacredness.
Rule the Queendom
you've been building.

Mariposa X Guerrera

Focus on what makes
you beautiful.
See yourself with
eyes of love.
Learn to see yourself
as the Creator does.
You are a breathtaking
piece of art.
Your imperfections are more beautiful than the stars.

Kim Guerra

Luche por mi
Libertad
por amor a mi misma.
Luche y gané.
Hoy volaré.

Mariposa X Guerrera

Believe women.
Stand with women.
Heal our women.

Kim Guerra

Estoy aprendiendo a respirar
a crecer como la flor
that grew from the concrete
through deserts of oppression
from fires and oceans.
I am stepping into my light
como el sol
setting and rising
todos los días.

Mariposa X Guerrera

Treat yourself como si fueras
tu flor favorita.
Get the light you need,
Nourish yourself,
Surround yourself with people and ideas
that help you grow.

Kim Guerra

I'm working on softening
my heart again.
I haven't had a reason to for a while,
but it's time to stop surviving.
Ya es tiempo to let myself live fully
to let myself feel the
full range of emotions
to let myself be gentle,
let las flores de mi corazón
grow once again.
Mi corazón está sanando
y floreciendo.

Mariposa X Guerrera

Cada mujer merece ser adorada,
chiquiada y valorada.
Si alguien no te hace sentir
como la reina que eres no te merece.

Live and learn homegirl.
Stop making excuses to not respect yourself.
Create beautiful things.
Drink water.
Work out and nourish your body.
Laugh loud.
Grow. Focus. Open your eyes.
Value the beauty
your soul has to offer this universe.

Mariposa X Guerrera

People
ask me why
I love butterflies.
I respond,
"They give themselves
wings."

Kim Guerra

Mujeres, we were raised believing
we need men to take care of us.
We were not taught to take care of ourselves.
Now, we are learning to believe
we are strong, smart, and powerful enough
to take responsibility for our vidas and dreams.
When a mujer believes in herself,
she raises herself like the sun.
She becomes her own source of light,
Alumbrando su propio mundo.
She becomes unstoppable,
Using nothing but her own luz to shine.

Mariposa X Guerrera

As hard as it may be,
let your heart soften.
Let the rock blossom
—a flor.
Keep your corazón
gentle.

Kim Guerra

Aprende a estar sola
a disfrutar de tu compañía.
Aprende que te hace
reír y llorar,
que te quita el aliento.
Aprende a enamorarte de la
persona que tú eres.
Aprende que tu corazón,
cuerpo, y espíritu
te acompañarán toda tu vida,
porque no conocerte
y amarte?

Escoge tu misma
como vas a dejar que te traten
otras personas.
Cómo te vas a tratar a ti misma.
¿Como reina o esclava?
Escoge ser poderosa.
No se te olvide que también puedes
ser tierna, inteligente, emprendedora.
Puedes ser lo que tú quieras.
Tu tienes el poder de escoger.

Kim Guerra

Our men have to do a lot better
Generations of men have had their toxic behaviors swept under the rug or met with
"Ya sabes cómo es"
"Pobrecito"
"Lo que pasa en la familia se queda en la familia"
We have been raised to fear el "que dirán" more
than La Llorona
The fear of holding men accountable has enabled our men to continue harmful patterns.
Mujeres in my family tell me Latin men come with their own warning labels.
"Ten cuidado con ellos, mija."
Mujeres, keep men accountable.
Hombres rise up to be the kings you were intended to be.

Mariposa X Guerrera

Today, I won.
I stepped on the scale,
the number had gone up.
My confidence
did not go down.
I loved myself the same.

Kim Guerra

Let the plants teach you.
A plant won't grow if it doesn't have
fertile soil to put down its roots.
Without roots from which to anchor and
absorb nutrients,
a flower will never bloom nor
a tree reach its full potential.
Light is necessary for plants and people,
a source of generous, life giving energy.
Water, dear ones, nourishes us,
cleanses us, and heals us.
Learn from the plants and
surround yourself with
elements, environments, and people
that will be a part of your growth
and not an excuse that keeps you from
Blooming.

Mariposa X Guerrera

Mujer, madre, magia
tu amor, como la tierra
sana
hace crecer y renacer.

Mujer, madre, magia
tus manos, como el sol
fortalecen
acarician y protegen.

Mujer, madre, magia
tus palabras, como el agua
alimentan
consuelan y renuevan.

Mujer, madre, magia
eres sagrada.

La luna te canta
el sol te fortalece
las estrellas brillan por ti.
Eres importante.
El universo no sería
igual sin ti.
Tu vida es sagrada,
tus sueños son necesarios.

Mariposa X Guerrera

Deep breaths and baby steps.
It is okay to take your time.
Give yourself space to feel
confident in your decisions.
Give yourself what it is you need.
Give yourself the opportunity
to face your fears.
Be generous with how you love
first yourself,
then others.
Deep breaths and baby steps.

Kim Guerra

I will throw my chancla at racistas y machistas.

Mariposa X Guerrera

El corazón
tiene el poder de crecer.
Our hearts heal
gather strength to
beat again.
Another miraculous
part of being
human.

Kim Guerra

When people of color gather
our golden ancestral threads weave
a revolutionary tapestry.
We share stories of oppression
we don't need to translate—
unspoken understanding.
We celebrate our strengths—
resilience.
We call out that gold
residing within us—
gold made of our ancestors'
sweat, tears, and blood.
People of color:
we are golden.

Mariposa X Guerrera

There is so much power
within you.
Society and toxic people
tried to take it from you.
Reclaim it, mariposa.
Reclaim the power
of your wings.
Surround yourself
with beings who
love you by
empowering you.

Kim Guerra

Speak your truth.
Stand your ground.
Set your boundaries.
Recognize your value—
Love yourself accordingly.

Mariposa X Guerrera

Life is a gift
given to us
daily.
Queen, fill it with
people and experiences
which make you feel
alive.
Tu vida es tuya
y de nadie más.

Kim Guerra

For every time you've doubted
yourself—
You are worthy of
believing in yourself.
For every time you've wanted
to give up—
You are worthy of
trying again.
For every time you've felt ashamed—
You are worthy of being loved.

Mariposa X Guerrera

Sentí mi corazón florecer
como una rosa
después del invierno.
Lo sentí latir con pasión
y tranquilidad
como las olas del océano.
Sentí mi corazón vivo
segura que aunque muera
seguirá latiendo.
Lo sentí pariendo—
Sentí amor naciendo de nuevo.

Kim Guerra

You are a sunflower, a ray of sol.
Eres una guerrera, a warrior mujer.
You are hermosa en todos los lenguajes.
Eres bilingue, eres badass.
No one can take away the words que tus parents
te enseñaron.
No one can take away los dichos, chistes,
y refranes.
Cuando hablamos Spanglish es como agregar
más colores a una obra de arte.
Cuando hablamos español es como una abrazo
al corazón—
Se siente como las manos de mi abuelita, llenas
de masa mientras hace tamales para Navidad.
Being Bilingual es como ser una tortilla rising.
Keep rising!

Mariposa X Guerrera

Believe Women.
As a survivor, I can't say how important it was to have people who believed me. People who stood by me, held me, and cried with me. It was healing to have people embrace me and not shame me. I needed people to tell me it was not my fault. The most painful moments are when people shame and blame the victim— simply because we were raised to protect and enable men. It's time to turn that patriarchal shit around, hold men accountable, and believe women the first time they speak their truths.

Kim Guerra

Mujer,
your story matters.
We were raised to cover up abuse,
and protect abusers.
You become a revolution
when you choose to
love yourself and believe
your voice, rights, and mental health
are important.
Mujer, your life matters.

Mariposa X Guerrera

Hold yourself like you'd hold a flower.
Be in awe of your own beauty—
the time you've taken to grow
the healing power held
within your color
the sweet aroma of a being
determined
to bloom.

Kim Guerra

I look in the mirror and see
a guerrera.
I see a mujer who has fought
for her vida and won.
I see a mujer determined to keep fighting
for herself, for mujeres, and for her people.
I see a mujer I am proud of.
I see a mariposa
getting used to having wings.
I see someone I love.

Mariposa X Guerrera

To all the light skinned Latines— it is our responsibility to acknowledge that we benefit from the societal standards and systems for having lighter skin/being white passing. This is a privilege our darker skinned Latines don't have. Lighter skinned Latines are over-represented in the media. Even in our homes the lighter skinned "güeritos" are seen as mas "bonitos". It is part of our responsibility to call out the colorism bullshit, honor our Latine hermanes with all sorts of melanin, and focus on empowering our people to keep rising. How are you owning and using your privilege?

Kim Guerra

Having privilege
should not be a source of division
amongst us hermanxs.
It's an opportunity to invite one another
to sit at the table.
If I have the queso fresco your tacos need,
I'm going to share it with you.
Just like you will share the horchata
I need when I'm thirsty.
Somos familia; somos hermanxs.
Que no se les olvide—
It's the most important part.

Mariposa X Guerrera

Mujer, estoy orgullosa de ti.
Tal vez hoy se te olvidó
que tienes alas.
I'm here to remind you
your wings are still there.
They tell the story of your
growth and transformation.
¡Que no se te olviden tus alas!

Kim Guerra

The most
powerful beings
in the world are
women who love
themselves.

Mariposa X Guerrera

I heard mujeres
sharing healing poems
with one another.
I saw Brown and Black mujeres
embracing one another,
wiping each other's tears.
We reminded each other of
our magia y fuerzas.
Esto es la revolución.

Kim Guerra

I believe you.

Mariposa X Guerrera

Las fuerzas de nuestra gente
son como las fuerzas del sol,
las ganas de las plantas creciendo,
y la firme ternura de la madre tierra.
Somos inigualables,
cada persona una estrella.
Juntos brillamos como una galaxia
alumbrando a este universo oscuro.

Kim Guerra

I am most unkind to myself
when I compare myself to others.
Las flores crecen
y saben que individualmente
son bellas
juntas
son jardines y campos de belleza.
We too,
are more beautiful when
we grow and bloom
together.

Mariposa X Guerrera

Ask your parents to tell you their stories.
They have immigration narratives,
trauma, abuse, and success
stored in their bones.
Their bodies know resiliency
intimately.
Look at the hands that raised you
they will tell you
your history.
Listen.

Kim Guerra

You are a
wildflower.
You grow in difficult places.
You absorb light and shine.
You are independent.
Florecita linda, florecita loca
solo necesitas tu alma
y la madre tierra
para florecer.

Mariposa X Guerrera

Use your voice and
state your needs
even when it's terrifying.
You have not fought this hard
to feel small again.
Your past, present, and future
self will thank you.

Kim Guerra

Domestic violence can be invisible
it can leave bruises only you know are there.
One person using their
power and control to rob another's
power and control.
Violence on another's emotional,
physical, spiritual, financia, political wellbeing.
It is an attack on a human being's fundamental rights.
I see you, beautiful human.
I believe you.
You are worthy of living in
freedom, safety, and love.

Mariposa X Guerrera

Sometimes
the scariest
thing about
love
is believing
we are worthy
of it.

Kim Guerra

Parte del amor es el perdón.
La paciencia para
aceptar las imperfecciones
es parte del arte de amar.
Ámate primero tú.
Perdónate primero tú.
Acepta tus imperfecciones.
Es la única manera que el amor crezca.

Mariposa X Guerrera

Something
sacred happens
when we honor
each other.

Kim Guerra

To our trans hermanes:
Y'all are mariposas
Winged beings
Transforming yourself
Into the most beautiful, authentic
Version of you.
Trans hermanes
Ustedes son magical humans
Brave enough to shine
Beyond the binary bullshit.
Your courage terrifies those
who are too scared to be themselves,
The ones who don't believe in magic.

Mariposa X Guerrera

El poder ya lo tienes
solo te falta creer
que tú puedes.
Believe you are worthy
of your fullest potential.
You are too badass
to not believe in your
own magic.

Kim Guerra

About the author

Kim Guerra is a queer woman of color. A butterfly woman who has given herself wings.

She is a writer, advocate, and entrepreneur. She is the creator of "Badass x Bonita", a brand and movement that she considers to be a work of self-love and her love for her community. She wants each person to wear "Badass x Bonita" products as a statement and shield-- a living revolution. Guerra is the author of "Mariposa" and "Mija": collections of bilingual poems, affirmations, and revolutionary love letters. "Badass x Bonita" is for all humans who are giving themselves and their community wings through revolutionary love.

She was born and raised in the San Fernando Valley in LA. Kim graduated from Cornell University and received her Masters in Marriage and Family Therapy from Antioch University in Seattle. She's currently based in Los Angeles and Coyoacán.

Kim Guerra

www.ingramcontent.com/pod-product-compliance
Lightning Source LLC
Chambersburg PA
CBHW072145100526
44589CB00015B/2103